THE POLITICS
OF SPIRITUALITY

By the same author

A Simplicity of Faith: My Experience in Mourning

Conscience and Obedience: The Politics of Romans 13 and Revelation 13 in Light of the Second Coming

An Ethic for Christians and Other Aliens in a Strange Land

A Second Birthday

My People Is the Enemy: An Autobiographical Polemic

Dissenter in a Great Society

Count It All Joy

Free in Obedience

Instead of Death

A Private and Public Faith

With Anthony Towne

The Death and Life of Bishop Pike

Suspect Tenderness

The Bishop Pike Affair

SPIRITUALITY AND THE CHRISTIAN LIFE
Richard H. Bell, *Editor*

THE POLITICS
OF
SPIRITUALITY

William Stringfellow

THE WESTMINSTER PRESS
Philadelphia

BOOK DESIGN BY ALICE DERR

First edition

Published by The Westminster Press®
Philadelphia, Pennsylvania

PRINTED IN THE UNITED STATES OF AMERICA
2 4 6 8 9 7 5 3 1

Library of Congress Cataloging in Publication Data

Stringfellow, William.
  The politics of spirituality.

  (Spirituality and the Christian life)
  1. Spiritual life—Anglican authors. 2. Christianity and politics. I. Title. II. Series: Spirituality and the Christian life series.
BV4501.2.S816 1984   248.4'83   84-10434
ISBN 0-664-24633-8 (pbk.)

FOR
GEORGE TODD

CONTENTS

EDITOR'S INTRODUCTION

In 1609 Francis de Sales published a helpful book designed "to instruct those who live in town, within families, or at court, and by their state of life are obliged to live an ordinary life." It was, as he said, "a collection of bits of good advice stated in plain, intelligible words." The book, *Introduction to the Devout Life*, became a "spiritual classic." Although we will not claim that the books in this series will become classics, they are intended for a similar reader—one "obliged to live an ordinary life"—and they are written in "plain, intelligible words."

In terms of their subject matter, they share another point with Francis de Sales's book. He said about the Christian life that "a strong, resolute soul can live in the world without being infected by any of its moods." This was not an easy task then, nor is it now. But one of the goals of the Christian life is to free ourselves from circumstances that hinder love and service to God. When the apostle Paul spoke of having the "mind of Christ," he was asking that we not yield to the accidental features of this world; that we strive to free ourselves from being defined by the social, political, and economic principalities and powers of this world. A great effort of the spirit is needed to do this.

This series is intended to help its readers in this effort of the spirit. We call these books spiritual because they deal with how God's Spirit intersects with the human spirit. They focus attention on the *Bible* as the principal source for hearing and understanding God's Spirit and on the *self* as part of a living, worshiping, and struggling community of God's people in this world.

Living in the spirit first involves seeing and facing the many ways in which we forget God in our everyday life. It means having courage to suffer the wounds meted out by our world. Beyond these things, living in the spirit is an active disposition—*a formation* of faith and *a practice* of gratitude and compassion before God. Spiritual formation and practice come as we remember God and share his presence in us with others.

If no other books you have read lately have encouraged you to take hold of your self and your Christian life with courage and firmness, these books will. They will take you patiently through many identifiable thickets of human life and ask you when it was that you allowed God to speak to you, and embrace you, and lead you. These books are intended to be traveling companions, guides to take you closer to the center of the Christian life, closer to the Bible, closer to yourself, and thus, it is hoped, closer to God.

This book, *The Politics of Spirituality*, and its companions in the series offer pathways for growing in the spirit. What may be only suggested in one book as a way of living as a Christian will be more richly developed in another. For example, both Stringfellow and

Bell, in *Sensing the Spirit,* discuss the dangers of self-indulgence and the material concerns of our worldliness,
notions alien to biblical spirituality. But while Stringfellow more prophetically confronts the secular powers
of this world, Bell leads the reader more gently through
the many ways we forget God in our life.

Stringfellow focuses our attention on what he calls
"biblical" spirituality, a spirituality rooted in the experience of discerning and partaking of the work of the
Word of God incarnate. Spirituality is the estate into
which people are baptized, says Stringfellow, and
which entitles the baptized person to be called saint.

Reaching for the heart of this biblical spirituality, Stringfellow points us to the concept of "holiness" and says
of it: being holy is "being whole . . . it means being liberated from religiosity and religious pietism of any sort;
it does not mean being morally better, it means being
exemplary; it does not mean being godly, but rather being truly human; it does not mean being otherworldly,
but it means being deeply implicated in the practical existence of this world without succumbing to this world
or any aspect of this world, no matter how beguiling."

After some characteristic polemics on our culture,
Stringfellow concludes that in the struggle against our
"dark age," where technocracy rules and humans are
robbed of both sanity and conscience, we must restore
two aspects of a "monastic" witness: intercession and
eucharistic praise. Complementary to this latter witness, Don Saliers in *Spirituality and Worship* explores
every detail of eucharistic praise in liturgy and in life.
For Saliers such praise sanctifies and restores our daily
life in Christ. Stringfellow develops these two concepts
as central to the political resistance of death. It is such

daily resistance to death that is the practice of biblical spirituality.

Those who are familiar with other books by William Stringfellow will not be surprised by his polemical style or his theology, but will find a fresh treatment of concepts like holiness, repentence, and judgment as these relate to our personal lives and the life of our nation and culture.

RICHARD H. BELL

THE AMBIVALENCE
OF "SPIRITUALITY"

He will cover you with his pinions,
and under his wings you will find refuge.
                                    Psalm 91

I had visited The College of Wooster, in Ohio, on several occasions over the years, to give lectures or to preach at the college church, and I had also spent an extended time there one semester as a theologian-in-residence. Hence I had come to know many of the Wooster faculty as colleagues and friends, and when Richard Bell, a professor in the department of philosophy at the college, initially sought me to contribute to this series of works on contemporary spirituality, I was receptive to the idea because it was Richard who bespoke it.

That circumstance helped to diminish certain qualms which I have long associated with the word "spirituality" and with a whole array of uses, innuendos, and connotations of the common language and popular idiom of "spirituality." I had confidence that Richard had recourse to the term with truthfulness, so far as a biblical perspective is concerned, free of the voguish, supercilious, commercialized, or religiose contexts in which "spirituality" and other words similar to it are invoked.

The ambivalence and, indeed, ambiguity of "spirituality"—especially in contemporary reference—is such that I seldom employ the term at all. I suspect "spirituality" is most often uttered as a ministerial deception, albeit often benignly intended. It then is a trick of clergy enabling something to be said when in truth there is nothing to say, or it is an ignorance equivalent to that. "Spirituality" is for many, particularly church folk, an intimidating term. It is recited authoritatively yet merely conceals a void. At the same time, it is rarely challenged in practice by listeners because they do not want to be considered obtuse "spiritually." There is, of course, a whole lexicon of words and phrases in common religious currency which have acquired similar auras and which regularly and successfully tempt preachers. The situation for the latter is something like the use of undefined professionalistic jargon by doctors or lawyers or generals when they have reason to evade or pretend or impress or otherwise take advantage of patients or clients or citizens. In any case, the common practice of resorting to such terms as spirituality in order to hide ignorance or mask incoherence or disguise a void immeasurably increases and complicates the inherent vagueness of the language of spirituality.

This whole matter of the elusive significance of so-called spirituality comes into acute focus, for me, in the cursory and profane regard which the name of the Word of God as the Holy Spirit suffers, more often than not, within the churches. I remember, for instance, that I was very impatient to be confirmed in the Episcopal Church. In my rearing as a child in that church I had come to think that confirmation was the occasion when the secrets were told. Confirmation, I supposed, was the event in which all the answers that had been previously withheld from me, because I was a child, would be forthcoming. In particular, I recall, I was eager to be confirmed because I expected in confirmation to learn the secret of the Holy Spirit. At last, I anticipated, my curiosity concerning this mysterious name would be satisfied.

In my experience as a child in the church, when adults named the Holy Spirit in the presence of children it was always an utterly obscure, unspecified, literally spooky allusion.

It did not specifically occur to me as a child to suspect that adults in the church did not in fact know what they were talking about when they used the name of the Holy Spirit. The reference, anyway, was always intimidating. The mere invocation of the name, without any definition, connection, or elaboration, would be effective in aborting any issues raised by a child. "The Holy Spirit" was the great, available, handy estopper.

Needless to say, confirmation turned out to be a great disappointment to me. I waited through catechism, but no secrets were confided. If anything, the name of the Holy Spirit was put to use in confirmation instruction with even deeper vagueness. On the day of confirmation I learned no secret except the secret that adults in the church had no secrets, at least so far as the Holy Spirit is concerned.

It was only later on, after I had begun to read the Bible seriously, on my own initiative, that the cloture about the Holy Spirit was disrupted and the ridiculous mystification attending *this* name of the Word of God began to be dispelled. In contrast to my childish impressions from experiences in church, I found the Bible to be definitive and lucid as to the identity, character, style, and habitat of the Holy Spirit. In the Bible, the Holy Spirit is no term summoned simply to fill a void, or to enthrall rather than instruct the laity, or to achieve some verbal sleight-of-hand because comprehension is lacking. Biblically, the Holy Spirit names the faithfulness of God to his own creation. Biblically, the Holy Spirit means the militant presence of the Word of God inhering in the life of the whole of creation. Biblically, the Holy Spirit is the Word of God at work both historically and existentially, acting incessantly and pervasively to renew the integrity of life in this world. By virtue of this redundant affirmation of the biblical witness, the false notion—nourished in my childhood in the Episcopal Church—that the Holy Spirit is, somehow, possessed by and enshrined within the sanctuary of the church was at last refuted, and I was freed from it. Coincidentally, as one would expect, the celebration in the sanctuary became, for me, authentic—a eucharist for the redemption of the life of the whole of creation in the Word of God—instead of vain ritual or hocus-pocus.

It was the biblical insight into the truth of the Holy Spirit that signaled my own emancipation from religiosity. It was the biblical news of the Holy Spirit that began, then, to prompt the expectancy of encounter with the Word of God in any and all events in the common life of the world and in my own life as a part of that. It was—it is—the biblical saga of the Word of God as Agitator, as the Holy Spirit, that assures me that wheresoever human conscience is alive and active, *that* is a sign of the saving vitality of the Word of God in history, here and now.

If the name of the Holy Spirit is manipulated or defamed throughout the churches (I consider my confirmation experience to be more typical than exceptional), then it is no wonder that "spirituality" and terms associated with "spirituality" would be recited in disjointed, self-serving, indefinite syntax. Somewhat ironically, there are not only these problems of vagueness and the like with the topic and vocabulary of "spirituality," but also those occasioned by a veritable plethora of references, allusions, or connections. "Spirituality" may indicate stoic attitudes, occult phenomena, the practice of so-called mind control, yoga discipline, escapist fantasies, interior journeys, an appreciation of Eastern religions, multifarious pietistic exercises, superstitious imaginations, intensive journals, dynamic muscle tension, assorted dietary regimens, meditation, jogging cults, monastic rigors, mortification of the flesh, wilderness sojourns, political resistance, contemplation, abstinence, hospitality, a vocation of poverty, nonviolence, silence, the efforts of prayer, obedience, generosity, exhibiting stigmata, entering solitude, or, I suppose, among these and many other things, squatting on top of a pillar.

The clutter associated with what is called spirituality is accentuated, if not fully or adequately explicated, by the frequent and familiar commercial exploitation of both the language and the subject of "spirituality" and, to use an appropriate technical term, the marketing of "spirituality" to mass constituencies inside the boundaries of American Christendom as well as outside those nominal precincts. The proliferation, in just the past two decades, of sects, therapies, cults, self-discovery movements, ashrams, and similar excursions is literally fantastic and betells a pathetic need which seems to be spawned in the culture itself. At the same time, these developments expose a poignant ridicule of the authentic spirituality vested in the church since the apostolic era and a colossal pastoral default chargeable to the churches. This has rendered "spirituality" vulnerable to commercialization and has caused the yearnings of human beings for spiritual integrity in living—as vague or diffuse as such may be—to be articulated in commercialized versions of the crudest degree.

Whether dominated by the profit motive or informed by some more beneficial attitude, the cults and sects and other enterprises instructing or demonstrating "spiritual" methods or techniques are, more often than not, intensely privatized. The concentration is usually upon self-realization of some sort disconnected with the rest of created life. Where that is the case, however appealing the "spirituality" exemplified may otherwise appear to be, the regime being sponsored or commended is categorically unbiblical. There is no biblical spirituality to be found in a vacuum, cut off from the remainder of humanity within the totality of creation. Indeed, biblical spirituality is significantly about the restoration or renewal of these relationships throughout the realm of created life. To put the same differently, biblical spirituality concerns living in the midst of the era of the Fall, wherein *all* relationships whatsoever have been lost or damaged or diminished or twisted or broken, in a way which is open to transcendence of the fallenness of each and every relationship and in which these very relationships are recovered or rendered new. This transfiguration wrought in biblical spirituality includes one's relationship with oneself, in the most self-conscious and radically personal sense, but it *simultaneously* implicates one concretely in reconciliation with the rest of creation and is thus *the most profoundly political reality available to human experience.* From a biblical perspective, therefore, the assertion of some species of so-called spirituality which is privatized and nonpolitical or antipolitical is, simply, nonsense. It is also, given the commercialization of much of what is called spirituality, a signal to beware of being exploited in more ways than one.

Biblical spirituality represents politics in the broadest possible scope and in a dimension which nurtures, locates, and matures the personal or the self. That is why, I think, the recall of Thomas Merton and his vocation is so lively in so many different places and for so many generations nowadays. It is also one of the reasons why so many alumni—or refugees—from the so-called activism of the decade of the sixties can be beheld today in spiritual pursuits. It is, in part, an endeavor to identify and articulate origins or roots and an effort to comprehend politics within the biblical scenario of creation and fall and redemption.

When all is said and done, however, the aspect of the ambivalence of contemporary "spirituality" that provokes me to be most wary, and has chiefly inhibited the use of such language in my own speaking and writing, is the popular interpretation of "spirituality" as a rejection of the most elementary teaching of the New Testament: the Incarnation. Where the syntax of "spirituality" refers to substance in content at all, and is not just some verbose mishmash, it often represents an emulation of the Greek mentality, or similar pagan attitude, in which the body is separated from the spirit, or the flesh from the soul, or the physical from the spiritual, the material from the mental, the tangible from the ethereal, and so on and on. These dichotomies—unbiblical, false, and basically deceptive—quickly lead to collateral distinctions equally offensive to the gospel of Jesus Christ, like those purporting to distinguish between the profane and the sacred, the secular and the sacrosanct, the temporal and the spiritual, the defiled and the pure. Whatever quaintness these juxtapositions may have poetically, theologically they are hostile to the truth of the Incarnation. This is, as far as I am concerned, not a matter of doctrine only. Primarily it is an issue of the denial inherent in such supposed dichotomies of the historic event of the implication of the Word of God in the common history of this world in Jesus Christ. It is in that event, it is in what has consummately happened in history in Jesus Christ, that all such separations are abolished.

The point is not esoteric but of immediate practical consequence: whatever else may be affirmed about a spirituality which has biblical precedent and style, spiritual maturity or spiritual fulfillment necessarily involves the *whole* person—body, mind, soul, place, relationships—in connection with the whole of creation throughout the era of time. Biblical spirituality encompasses the whole person in the totality of existence in this world, not some fragment or scrap or incident of a person. This book has no other aim than to commend, thus, the efficacy of the Incarnation.

That means, of course, my own effort in this writing is (mercifully) modest and, I trust, straightforward, not esoteric, and, because of the ambivalence of contemporary "spirituality," necessarily redundant.

The Incarnation, as that is vested and manifested in Jesus Christ, renders Christ the exemplary human being. Christ is the person not only identified and fulfilled within himself but simultaneously reconciled in the Word of God with the whole of created life in this world. One implication of this event in Christ for the rest of humanity is the prospect of encounter with the Word of God in the common life of the world which it anticipates and the possibility for human beings to thereby affirm the Word of God in terms of their own experience in *any* circumstances. It is the same truth of the Incarnation which enables human beings to discern the active presence of the Word of God in the world without succumbing to the temptation of becoming conformed to the world.

The secret of that capability of being in but not of the world originates in fidelity to the gospel. What is important is faithfulness to the reality of the Incarnation, rather than anxiety over so-called effectiveness or success or similar purposes which, however attractively disguised, are in fact worldly aspirations signifying the tyranny of death feigning to reign in this world in the place of the sovereignty of the Word of God embodied in Jesus Christ.

This is why I have herein invoked some of the psalms, not as material for exegesis but, rather, for use as prayers. Despite all the variety and diversity of experience and experiment identified, in some sense, as spirituality, I am quite content to leave all that to one side and to be, instead, attentive to the psalms. I mean I am open to letting the psalms define spirituality and the appropriate and authentic scope, topic, range, posture, action of a spiritual style of life. More than that, the psalms rehearse every need, every desire, every complaint, every appeal, every mood, every experience of every sort, and thus one turns to the psalms to be prompted or inspired, edified or prodded, reminded or consoled. And that represents enough spiritual exercise for anyone.

I had little appreciation of the cogency of the psalms from my church upbringing. Their use was more or less confined to liturgical practice, and that was usually tedious and difficult to hear with comprehension. In later years, outside of church sanctuaries, I found myself turning with progressive frequency to the psalms in, I suppose, a certain desperation occasioned by my own recurrent, protracted, abrasive harassments of pain. I do not mean that I have used the psalms to distract myself from such pain as I live in from day to day, but rather I find that the psalms are a virtually inexhaustible consolation to me because they express already what I need to confront and confess concerning my frailty.

As it happens, this book is being written during a period in which I endure almost continuous and very aggravated pain. (I wonder how that fact affects my theology.) So, simultaneously with the effort of the book, I have been spending a lot of time with the psalms. And some few of them I cite here to shape the manuscript, though not, as I have said, to exegete, since, anyway, I do not think it apt (or even possible) to exegete a psalm.

I recognize, of course, that the present episode of pain has, conceivably, a direct relevance to the subject of this book. In earlier times, it was often supposed that spirituality involved mortification of the flesh. I find little biblical warrant for such practices, especially those which seem physically bizarre or those which were self-inflicted; I suspect much of all this was in fact inverted self-indulgence. Whatever the truth in the earlier circumstances, the event of the pain I suffer while composing this book, albeit not self-induced, is some sort of mortification of my flesh. I am not in a position to assess the significance of that, even though I can recognize this implication of mortification in the pain which lately visits me.

It has been my fortune to do the final composition of this book during the winter–spring semester of 1984, while I have been in residence at the General Theological Seminary in New York City. I am grateful for the hospitality of the seminary and the concern of the seminary community, as well as being glad for the reestablishment of many relationships which had originated during my sojourn in East Harlem in the fifties and sixties. At the same time I am thankful for the patience and practical assistance of Daniel Wetmore, who had also been much help to me here and, during the past two years, while I have been in fragile or perilous health at home on Block Island. And I wish to acknowledge the care that I have had from Harold Markus, M.D., and his holistic medical associates. All of these, and some others, share responsibility for the perseverance of which this book is evidence.

This, then, is a treatment of spirituality as an elementary political reality. To reiterate, by speaking of politics in connection with spirituality I am affirming what I understand to be the familiar biblical insight into the realm of the spiritual, as that may be contrasted with or opposed to other forms or varieties of spirituality. Politics, hence, refers comprehensively to the total configuration of relationships among humans and institutions and other principalities and the rest of created life in this world. Politics describes the work of the Word of God in this world for redemption and the impact of that effort of the Word of God upon the fallen existence of this world, including the fallen life of human beings and that of the powers that be. Politics points to the militance of the Word of God incarnate, which pioneers the politics of the Kingdom which is to come. Politics heralds the activity of the Word of God in judgment over all persons and all regimes and all things whatsoever in common history.

Spirituality, as far as I am given now to understand it, represents the *ordinary* experience of discerning and partaking in these politics. It is that very estate into which people are baptized. It is the same circumstance which, in the origins of the church of Jesus Christ, entitled every baptized person to be called *saint*. So it was, long ago. In truth, so it is today.

William Stringfellow

The Day of Saint Matthias, 1984

THE POLITICS
OF SPIRITUALITY

CHAPTER ONE

WORLDLINESS
AND HOLINESS

Clap your hands, all peoples!
Shout to God with loud songs of joy!
For the LORD, *the Most High, is terrible,*
a great king over all the earth.

Psalm 47

There are obvious ways to deal with the ambivalence attending the idiom of "spirituality" about which I so much complain in the preface. One is to conclude that "spirituality" is so damaged as a term by religiosity, commercialization, vagueness, ambiguity, superficiality, self-indulgence, and other problems that it should just be abandoned. I have much sympathy for that view, and, as I have mentioned, I seldom have used the word "spirituality" in my other books or in articles, sermons, or lectures.

Another option is to modify "spirituality" with some definitive reference. This is what I have already done here, in the phrase *biblical spirituality*, in order to indicate a spiritual disposition, experience, or practice which has precedent or exemplification in the biblical chronicle, as in the Acts of the Apostles, or which is otherwise informed or prompted by the style or substance of the biblical witness, as in the Psalms. The virtue of this is that it at least clarifies the sorts of so-called spirituality that are *not* being considered.

If, alternatively, one substitutes other terms in place of "spirituality," I commend "santification" or "holiness." While I do not wish to magnify semantic or rhetorical issues, or to dwell much on them, both sanctification and holiness bring freight and are often subject to inflated connotations. In any case, by sanctification I mean the endeavor by which a person is sanctified or rendered holy. The endeavor is not one of the person so affected but, quite the contrary, is an effort of the Word of God, which *elects* the one made holy and which, I believe, offers similar election freely to every person. To be more precise about it, *sanctification is a reiteration of the act of creation in the Word of God.* Thus sanctification refers to the activity of the historic Word of God renewing human life (and all of created life) in the midst of the era of the fall, or during the present darkness, in which the power of death apparently reigns. Holiness designates the essential condition of a person who confesses that he or she has suffered the renewal of his or her being, or selfhood, in the Word of God and is restored to wholeness as a human being. While there *is* an implication, in being holy, of incessant repentance, there is no implication of perfection or of any superior moral status. Among humans, holiness may involve a relatively more profound experience of being human, but it does not indicate as such the exceptional or the extraordinary. To the contrary, holy connotes the holistic in human life and, in that connection, the normal, the typical, the ordinary, the generic, the exemplary.

The Irony of Being Holy

I am aware, of course, that sanctification is ridiculed and holiness is belittled—and the saints are defamed and scandalized—when especial moral worth or purity or achievement is imputed to being holy. This is in reality a condescension of those conformed to the world, their form of dismissal, an excuse for others to cop out in a manner which pretends to recognize and flatter the saints.

Within my own memory, probably the outstanding incident of this pretentiousness happened on the day in 1970 when Daniel Berrigan (the Jesuit who had become both celebrated and notorious for his resistance to the war in Southeast Asia), then being sought by the federal authorities as a fugitive (as Dan puts it) from injustice, was seized by the FBI at the home of Anthony Towne and myself on Block Island. The event was heavily covered by television and other media, and that evening, on one of the Providence TV newscasts, an interview was conducted, about Dan's capture, with another prominent Jesuit who was in the jurisdiction. He was John J. McLaughlin, a candidate in the Republican Party for the United States Senate. This was, of course, before strictures against priests in public office were widely pronounced by the Pope. (McLaughlin lost and later achieved some prominence on the White House staff as casuist for President Nixon, but after a while he quit the Jesuit order.) In the interview on television the day that Dan was seized, Father McLaughlin delivered a long and verbose comment about those who work for change from within the system and those who work for change from outside the system. But then, as if summing up the contrast, he declared, "Of course, you must remember that Dan is a poet!" With that accusation, he not only dismissed the Berrigan witness against the Vietnam war but also banished Dan from the company of ordinary folk. Dan is different from other people: Dan is a poet: Dan is eccentric: what applies to Dan does not have relevance or weight for other persons. More than that, at the conclusion of this sophistry is the notion that because a poet is considered idiosyncratic, an ordinary human (i.e., a non-poet) is excused from the claims of conscience which may be thought to influence the poets.

McLaughlin's evasion of conscience aside, as I have stressed being holy, becoming and being a saint does not mean being perfect but being whole; it does not mean being exceptionally religious, or being religious at all, it means being liberated from religiosity and religious pietism of any sort; it does not mean being morally better, it means being exemplary; it does not mean being godly, but rather being truly human; it does not mean being otherworldly, but it means being deeply implicated in the practical existence of this world without succumbing to this world or any aspect of this world, no matter how beguiling. Being holy means a radical self-knowledge; a sense of who one is, a consciousness of one's identity so thorough that it is no longer confused with the identities of others, of persons or of any creatures or of God or of any idols.

For human beings, relief and remedy from such profound confusion concerning a person's own identity and the identity and character of the Word of God becomes the indispensable and authenticating ingredient of being holy, and it is the most crucial aspect of becoming mature—or of being fulfilled—as a human in this world, in fallen creation. This is, at the same time, the manner through which humans can live humanly, in sanity and with conscience, in the fallen world as it is. And these twin faculties, sanity and conscience—rather than some sentimental or pietistic or self-serving notion of moral perfection—constitute the usual marks of sanctification. That which distinguishes the saint is not eccentricity but sanity, not perfection but conscience.

These are all considerations which impinge upon why I commonly use, herein, and have used, for more than a decade, in other books or public utterances, the *Word of God* as the name of God, in preference to the mere term *God*.

In American culture, and, I suspect, everywhere else, the name of God is terribly maligned. For one thing the name *God* is seldom any longer used as a name, and that in itself is a literal curse addressed to God. To take a very obvious and familiar example, when Ronald Reagan, in his pronouncements on the school prayer issue and otherwise, says "God," it is difficult to fathom what he may be fantasizing, though it would appear, at most, that he is imagining some idea of god. Sometimes he himself clarifies that by inserting a prefix and speaking of "his god" or "our god" or, also, "their god," while mentioning, as Reagan perceives the situation, an alien or enemy people.

Yet *no* idea of god is God; no image of god is God; no conception of god, however appealing or, for that matter, however true, coincides with the living God— which the biblical witness bespeaks—present, mani-

fest, militant in common history, discernible in the
course of events through the patience and insight of ordinary human beings. The living God, whose style and
character the Bible reports, is subject now, as in the biblical era, to the witness of human beings, to their tes-
timony describing what they have beheld of the intent,
involvement, self-disclosure, effort, and concern of the
Word of God in this world. And so, with as much
standing or authority as our predecessors in the faith
had long ago, biblical people in this day attest to God,
as he is revealed in this history, as the *Word of God,* the
very same One to whom the biblical witness refers and
in which the biblical witness so much rejoices.

When, therefore, I use here this name of God, it is
deliberately intended to invoke the scriptural saga of
the Word of God active in common history from the
first initiative of creation. Simultaneously I refer (as, so
to say, both Isaiah and John insist), the selfsame Word
of God incarnate in Jesus Christ. At the same time, I
mean to recall the Word of God permeating the whole
of creation and ready to be discerned in all things whatsoever in the fallenness of this world; and, again, the
Word of God as the Holy Spirit, at work contempora-
neously, incessantly agitating change in this world (as
the event of Pentecost and the Acts of the Apostles each
verify).

The restoration of the original identity of a person—
in all its particularities and all its relationships, in the
totality of its political significance—the renewal of a
person's wholeness, which is the initiation into holiness, is utterly the effort of the Word of God. There is
no interpretation which is attributable to a person's ambition, attainment, discipline, works, or merit. The re-

newal of creation, including the restoration of integrity to persons, is a matter of the grace of the Word of God. It is a generous gift indeed, as I have already mentioned, encompassing the restoring of relationships within a person and between that person and all other persons, all principalities and powers, nature, and the residuum of creation. The gift is also precocious because it is offered *now,* in the midst of the fall, in a way that disrupts, challenges, and resists the apparent sovereignty of the power of death in this world. That means, in turn, that this is an experience which shatters time and liberates people from the confinement of time by at once recalling all that has gone before and anticipating all that is to come.

Instead of being somehow transported "out of this world," rather than indulging abstinence, evasion, or escapism, rather than fabricating some isolation or separation or privatism, the irony in being holy is that one is plunged more fully into the practical existence of this world, as it is, than in any other way.

Spirituality as Conformity to This World

The irony of being holy contains, of course, no surprising news; it is no more than a manner of stating the New Testament enjoinder for those who follow Jesus to be in the world but not of the world.

An implication of the call to live in the world as it is with utter vulnerability—even, indeed, unto the risk of death—and an implication of the rejection of any notion of spirituality as some kind of super piety, yields a second or parallel irony. Commercialized or religiose or

other ersatz forms of spirituality typically require conformity to the world and avail no freedom from conformity to the regime of the world, even though they
boast their own spiritual jargon or assert transcenden-
tal goals. Such conformity, though it may assume attractive guises, as was the case for Jesus when he was
confronted by the power of death in the wilderness, *always* means conformity to death. And, as the experience of Jesus verifies, the issue in such temptations is
not one of merely compromising principle; the issue is
becoming an idolator of the power of death.

Without making pretentious judgments, it is possible
to discern where conformity, in this latter sense, is involved and to identify some marks that betell this in the
sects and movements and other enterprises claiming to
extol and teach "spirituality."

One telltale mark is where some version of the great
American success ethic is manifest. Some of the so-
called gospel businessmen's groups are representative
of this. Their appeal is that the Lord will somehow in-
duce material success in sales and merchandising or the
like. Or, they claim, "prayer" will achieve comparable
commercial dividends. One finds a plethora of similar
examples among the religious telecasts. The *700 Club*—
modeled after the most successful pagan TV talk
show—is a seemingly endless parade of testimonies
about the instantaneous rewards, of a tangible and usually material character, visited upon someone who has
attained the spiritual status that the program propa-
gates. The main emphases are upon one's effort or
accomplishment and, then, the rewards promptly furnished in the form of prosperity, fame, purported healing, promotion, publicity, or whatnot. Meanwhile,

there is no mention of Jesus in the wilderness episode I have referred to above, or of his repeated admonitions against notoriety and coveting notoriety, or of his poverty and the similar vocations of his disciples and the community of the Apostolic Church, or of his most ignominious execution, in a manner usually reserved for insurrectionists—in a manner, in other words, that was deemed a disgrace per se. Is Jesus on the cross, in worldly terms, a success? Yet in the precincts of the famous *700 Club*, the truth about Jesus as the world's greatest failure, or about Jesus who, according to the devil, could have had it all, so far as wealth and power and success are concerned, is, simply, suppressed in favor of these vulgar stories about instant tangible success for the converts.

I do not desire, in naming the *700 Club* specifically as an example of the spiritual hucksterism prevalent on television, to be critical only of that program. I cite the *700 Club* because it is the most deeply and audaciously profane of the current telecasts that I have audited. It would not surprise me to encounter something even more bold. The reason there are so many, the reason this genre of pseudo-spirituality proliferates, is, as far as I can discern, because these essentially are commercial enterprises and merchandising organizations, having nothing to do with biblical faith or biblical spirituality. One concrete evidence of that is the fact that these success stories are presented on the program in question as if they constituted some proof of the existence, and disposition, of God. That is a style of god talk distant indeed from the biblical testimonies reporting the activity of the Word of God in common history; as distant as Babel.

Another startling omission in "spirituality" quarters such as these is mention of the fall and of the significance of the fall. To be sure, in the personal anecdotes presented there will almost invariably be a recitation of private sin, predictably implicating one or another of the conventional vices or prosaic lusts—sex, booze, drugs, etc., etc. Such matters are encompassed within the purview of the fall. But the fall means far more than that. The fall refers to the profound disorientation, affecting all relationships in the totality of creation, concerning identity, place, connection, purpose, vocation. The subject of the fall is not only the personal realm, in the sense of you or me, but the whole of creation and each and every item of created life. The fall means the reign of chaos throughout creation now, so that even that which is ordained by the ruling powers as "order" is, in truth, chaotic. The fall means a remarkable confusion which all beings—principalities as well as persons—suffer as to who they are and why they exist. The fall means the consignment of all created life, and of the realm of time, to the power of death.

To understate or otherwise diminish the reality of the fall radically distorts not only the corpus of the confession of biblical faith but also the comprehension of biblical folk of the world as it is and of that which is involved in the redemption of the world. Suffice it here to say that the biblical description of the fall liberates people to view this world with unflinching, resilient realism. That is part of the ethos in which the judgment of the Word of God takes place. At the same time, that same realism is an indispensable credential for witness and ministry, for *any* witness or *any* ministry at all. And, perhaps most urgent, that same realism, with which, as Ephesians might say, the saints are equipped in their understanding of the fall, is the very threshold of hope. It is, to notice another irony, that which enables living in this world in hope.

What I am saying, of course, in part, is that much of what is asserted to be "spirituality" is utterly alien to biblical spirituality and is, in truth, no more than nihilism. It is a form of idolatry of death and sometimes, more particularly, an idolatry of the fear of death. In any case, it is a worship of *nothing*—a fascination with *no thing*, a heavily conditioned, self-conscious, circular pursuit of nothing, an elevation of nonexistence, a truly and appropriately chaotic endeavor, a glorification, finally, of the genius of the power of death. Among the most widespread symptoms of this morbid effort are the frantic preoccupations—endemic now in American culture—with security and survival. More often than not these manifestations are exposed as nihilistic because they are accompanied by defamation and persecution of the underclasses of society, notably the dispossessed and the homeless.

Nihilism offers no hope for living, but it contrives some substitutes for hope. Perhaps the most familiar is hedonism. In place of hope there is immediate gratification, usually sensual or material, and commonly in gross proportions far beyond immediate human needs. That is one reason why gluttony has become a prime social and personal problem in this culture, even though the churches seem steadfast in their apathy about it, and the ruling economic, commercial, and political powers seem equally determined to encourage and increase gluttony as if it were some civic virtue.

Nihilism is, at the same time, a frequent sponsor of

nostalgia as a substitute for hope. This is a heavy commercial fad. It may bear little or no correspondence to
the historical truth, but it serves to fill the void where
ideology articulates no hope and it condones carrying
nostalgia into fantasy dimensions.

Such devices and deceptions as these abet the insu-
lation of people from the realism of living in the midst
of the fall with some sense of humanity, for themselves and in relationships. Then, after a while, the hu-
manizing faculties malfunction and fail; they become so
suppressed or neglected as gifts of life that they atro-
phy. And so it seems that nihilism signifies a triumph
of death over life, spreading its own idolatry.

Self-denial as Self-indulgence

The regimens of much professed contemporary spirituality or those of various brands of pseudo-spirituality dwell upon self-denial or self-suppression as a basic
secret for attaining the state of selfhood sought through
a particular "spiritual" practice. Within the churches,
preachers are notorious in spreading the impression
that some such experience of self-denial is requisite to
gaining "spiritual" status. When pressed for specifics
about such supposed chastenings, these same preachers, in my observation, are seldom able to go beyond
an advocacy of surrendering bad habits, usually related
to one or another of the common appetites. I hear little
from these same quarters about repentance or renewal
of persons or restoral of life. That comes as no special
surprise, since the whole notion of self-denial or suppression of self, associated with a purported spiritual-

ity, is really a matter of self-indulgence, a vainglorious idea, a superficial "spiritual" exercise at most.

I reiterate what has heretofore been affirmed—and what will again and again be affirmed—in this book: Holiness is not an attainment, in any sense of the term, but is a gift of the Word of God. Holiness is not a badge of achievement for a saint but is wrought in the life, in the very being, of an ordinary person by the will of the Word of God. Holiness, from the vantage of the person who may truthfully be said to be holy, is, in the most elementary meaning, the restoration of integrity and wholeness to a person. That inherently involves, for that person, repentance—utter repentance, encompassing and comprehending the whole of that person's existence, even recollecting one's creation in the Word of God by the Word of God. It involves, as well, a prospective or continuing living in repentance unto the very day of the Judgment of the Word of God in the consummation of the history of this world. But such radical repentance does not imply, much less require, self-denial or any sort of suppression or sublimation of self. Quite the contrary: In becoming and being sanctified, *every* facet, feature, attribute, and detail of a person is exposed and rejuvenated, rendered new as if in its original condition again, and restored. Thus, instead of self-denial, what is taking place is more nearly the opposite of self-denial: in place of denial there is fulfillment.

The experience of Saint Paul is edifying in this respect, particularly since Paul has furnished us with more news of his experience in becoming and being a saint than any other New Testament character. To take a straightforward example, Paul in his early career

boasted that he was the most zealous of those who per-
secuted the gospel and confessors of the gospel. From
that we know that Paul had a quality, perchance even
talent, which is described as *zeal*. Later on, Paul becomes the most zealous apologist for the gospel, even
aspiring to confront the Emperor with his advocacy. Lo!
Paul retains this quality of zeal, save now, when he has
become the great apologist, this aspect of his person-
hood is turned around, renewed, matured, restored to
him in something like its original integrity in his own
creation in the Word of God. The zeal of Paul does not
have to be excised in order for him to become and be a
saint, although he had engaged this zeal of his to har-
ass and harm and inhibit the gospel. Had his zeal been
somehow suppressed or extinguished, it would then
have been less than the person Paul implicated in con-
version and in becoming holy. And *that* becomes a self-
contradiction: It is only the whole person, fully repent-
ant, without anything withheld, denied, secreted, who
can be holy.

The Political Character of Biblical Spirituality

Most forms of so-called spirituality which are pietistic assert that they are nonpolitical or apolitical. Some
boast that they are antipolitical, which is curious, since
the antipolitical *itself* is always a certain narrow kind of
politics. In any case, in one way or another the matter
of personal spirituality and its attainment is posed
against the political and the political is rejected. With-
drawal or abstention from the political realm in consequence of some such categorical rejection of the politi-

cal is a clue, practically conclusive in itself, that the spirituality being propagated is ersatz. It certainly is not connected with the biblical witness. Biblical spirituality is political in the most comprehensive, even cosmic sense, as I have earlier affirmed, expressing the politics of the Kingdom or signifying the effort of the Word of God in this world to redeem this world—the politics of redemption.

There is, in short, a political character to biblical spirituality which sets it apart from any professed spirituality which is apolitical or nonpolitical, as well as antipolitical, and that political character of biblical spirituality originates or has authority in the politics of the gospel itself.

That the biblical news has political content is evident in the herald of John the Baptist to the advent of Jesus, but the matter has a broader context than that. The Magnificat, for instance, reminds us of the political significance of the coming of Jesus and identifies the event with the foresight and anticipation of Isaiah. The psalms, of course, are replete with political references in setting forth images of the Judgment of the Word of God over the nations and over all things as the consummate political happening, to which all other politics, of whatever emphasis or mode, point.

Moreover, as Jesus comes into the world, the politics attending his coming become very mundane and concrete. The journey to Bethlehem, for one thing, was an enforcement of a policy of surveillance of an occupied people on the part of the incumbent authorities. The gathering at the manger of the shepherds, and various creatures, and the kings and the homage to the new king represented there not only exemplify the sovereignty of the Word of God in this world vested in Jesus as Lord of creation and history but also preview his office as Judge in the consummation of the age that is vouchsafed. The manger scene is not some quaint pastoral picture, a Sunday school tale for the children, except in circumstances where it has been thoroughly secularized and profaned, such as in the Pawtucket city hall crèche under the authority of the Justice Burger's simple majority on the bench of the United States Supreme Court. The manger story apprehends the Judgment and explicates how the Judgment impinges *now* upon the nations and the rulers of the nations.

Moreover, the examples are profuse in the life of Jesus as to the political dimension of the gospel. Consider Herod's attempt to assassinate the child. Or the healing episodes in which Jesus directly confronts the demonic powers and their effort to wreck creation and ruin human life. And notice how all these specific incidents culminate in that agonizing encounter in the wilderness in which Jesus is tempted by the power of death incarnate as the devil in explicit political terms. I sometimes receive the impression in church that people suppose that Jesus, in the wilderness, was practicing yoga exercises. There was no such thing, according to the witness that has come to us biblically. Jesus in the wilderness was tempted, truly tempted, to become idolatrous of the power of death, thereby rejecting the very Word of God which constituted his being. He transcends and repels the temptations and thus enunciates his Lordship in this world now. *That* politics is, then, verified in his crucifixion. The politics of the gospel are the politics of the cross.

That means, manifestly, that the politics of biblical

spirituality involve the renunciation of worldly power and the condiments that commonly are associated with worldly power: wealth or the control thereof, success, fame, applause, ambition, avarice, goals, competitive esprit, and the rest of the success syndrome. Biblical spirituality means powerlessness, living without embellishment or pretense, free to be faithful in the gospel, and free from anxiety about effectiveness or similar illusions of success.

It means living within the ironic aspects of holiness, equipped with that realism grounded in the biblical insight into the fallenness of the whole of creation. It means acting politically in a manner which confesses insistently, patiently, fearfully, joyously that Jesus Christ *is* the Lord and that the Lord already reigns.

That is why I consider that the politics of biblical spirituality are, beyond every comparison, the most radical politics of all.

CHAPTER TWO

JUSTICE AND JUSTIFICATION

O LORD, how long shall the wicked,
how long shall the wicked exult?
Psalm 94

The most significant flaw, from a biblical perspective, in the various pagan varieties of "spirituality"—whether prompted by commercial agendas or religious fervor or super pietism or private soul-searching—is that they each misconstrue and misrepresent the issue of justification.

Justification refers to how a person enters a sense of moral worthiness, a conviction of identity and vocation, a sustained experience of being whole and holy. The wisdom of the New Testament is that a justified state is not some moral status achieved by the enthusiasm or enterprise of a person but is a grace bestowed upon one by the Word of God. Justification is not something anyone deserves or can earn. It is not a matter of merit; it is a matter of election, an aspect of the discretion of the Word of God. Christians affirm that such discretion or the offer of election extends to the whole of humanity throughout the present age. The pagan modes of "spirituality" focus upon the initiative that someone must undertake in pursuit of justification, but biblical spirituality insists that the initiative belongs to the Word of God alone and that it is a gratuitous initiative, the generosity of which will not be fully disclosed until the Judgment. Furthermore, biblical spirituality, as a matter of practice, calls upon a person to surrender every attempt, including those subtle ones, to justify oneself. Nothing inhibits the grace of the Word of God more stubbornly and more commonly than challenging or contesting the initiative that is the grace of the Word of God.

Part of what is involved here is the freedom of a person to be herself or himself and to accept and love one's wholeness as a person. That contemplates acceptance of all one deems "good" but, at the same time, all one considers "bad." One accepts all of oneself without presuming to judge oneself. And, it should go without saying, one does not accede to the judgment of society, or of the church, or of the family, or whatever; one does not conform to such surrogate pretenses at judgment.

A person becomes justified by trusting the Judgment of the Word of God in all things whatsoever.

The Judgment of the Word of God over this world and all that are in it is a matter of grace, and not some minor grace but the consummate grace that recalls, anticipates, and completes all incidents of grace.

A Vain Anxiety for Justification

In American culture and in the churches of the contemporary culture, as well as among the assorted cults and sects and other enterprises fostering pagan "spirituality," there is an anxiety concerning justification which is at once pervasive and incessant. That such can be said to be manifest in the churches at all is a pathetic circumstance and one gauge to how much the churches are conformed in this culture to this culture. In any case, a plethora of illustrations, verifying such conformity and indicating issues in the culture as such, claims attention.

The preeminence accorded youth in America carries within it connotations of justification. The one who is young, attractive physically, bursting with energy, sexually provocative, and ready, athletic, overcompensated, cool, fashionable, laid back, and the like is accounted as morally worthy, deserving especially of self-esteem and, in turn, the admiration or envy of others. And hence there is, and has been for quite a long time in this culture, an overemphasis on youth and the appurtenances and appearances of youth; upon attaining youth and retaining youth. This idolatry of youth, compounded as it may be of the most literally superficial aspects of age and style, nevertheless has very wide appeal, even where it occasions oppression or persecution of the generations that are not young. Most conspicuous is perhaps the consignment of the elderly to limbo by legislating retirement and then providing for most of them only a choice among forms of custody or confinement—retirement villages, nursing homes, hospitals, public institutions—where the "old" are consigned to await death. A common premise of this process seems to be to keep the elderly out of sight, so that mainline society, the society of the young, can exist without intrusion of the outcast older people. It is a cruel attitude that has come to pass. After all, confinement and invisibility of the elderly is, in principle, a policy of elimination, and only some few steps away from the barbarities of extermination.

Behind the dominance of youth in the culture are notions of justification: that youth is superior, practically and morally, and to be old is inferior; that youth is effectual, but to be elderly is to be ineffectual; that youth means health, but age means infirmity; that youth anticipates success, but to grow old is failure; that youth deserves esteem, but to be old is a matter of embarrassment or shame. And so youth flourishes, or so it seems, but the elderly are put aside, out of sight, neglected and ignored as if, in these ways, to hasten death for them.

One can say, of course, very much the same thing about other classes or groups in this society. The handicapped, disabled, retarded, and, in many, many instances, the ill are treated with similar discrimination while being, essentially, discarded by society. There is, for one example, persuasive evidence that about two hundred thousand babies are victims of homicide at the hands of doctors and, sometimes, parents because they are at birth medically pronounced deformed or retarded. Part of the rationalization for such illicit euthanasia is the devaluation suffered by any life in this culture, if it varies noticeably from the stereotype of youth—and success, capability, beauty, health—which the culture sponsors.

Somewhat ironically, the span of youth is being shortened. On one end the social definitions of the elderly expand in various ways, especially in regard to the terms and conditions of retirement and unemployability, while on the other end, childhood is also curtailed. The oppression of children in America frequently means that a child is placed in home and preschool in circumstances that do not afford space or time or opportunity for the child to be a child. The pressures are to grow up quickly, and thus to become competitive, to be precocious about work, to play at games which are occupationally indoctrinating, to refrain from idleness or daydreaming or otherwise wasting time. But there seems to be little freedom for the child in this premature rat race, and the outcome is the rendering of clones with nothing to make up for the loss, in the process, of the imagination and adventure of childhood.

As it appears to me, Americans do not much nurture their children any longer; they deny or circumscribe the right to be a child and then brutalize the children.

The anxiety for justification illustrated by the idolatry of youth and the discard of the elderly is but an example. Many more might be cited. The consumption ethic that has emerged, especially in the period since the end of the Second World War, has heavy connotations of the same anxiety. The notion there is that the morally worthy are those who have the facility to consume in an open-ended, indefinite—indeed, indiscriminate—manner, without regard to their empirical need and without respect for the needs of other human beings. This is consumption for the sake of consumption; it is profligate consumption. The capability that sustains it is not wealth, in the traditional sense of tangible assets, but instead the receipt of compensation (more than likely unrelated to productive work) and access to credit. The corollary to this conviction that consumption is the index of moral worth is the opinion, so widely circulated within the Reagan administration, that the unemployed and uncompensated, the homeless, the dispossessed, the hungry, the welfare recipients, the disabled are somehow morally defective, indolent or dishonest or inherently inferior; in short, unjustified.

The implication of justification in the operation of the consumption ethic is, obviously, greatly accentuated by the conspicuous incidents of much consumption—clothes, cars, gadgets, appliances, playthings—and the whole scheme of consumption in American society supplies the basis for hedonism or self-gratification as a pseudo-spirituality.

Meanwhile, the effort and attention expended in consumption per se represents a diversion from other issues, so that consumption becomes a vicarious and highly political activity, even where it is masked as a private or personal pursuit. And, as has already been implied, it sponsors indifference and apathy, often of cruel dimensions, toward those excluded from the realm of the consumption ethic. That is why, of course, I am caustic about the *700 Club*, which so often upholds the consumption ethic as an ideal or even as a reward for the "justified."

The Mythology of a "Justified" Nation

The American anxiety concerning justification is not a merely private matter but has manifold political ramifications. Perhaps the most notorious political consequence of this anxiety, expressed on a societal and cultural level in openly political terms, is the mythology (not to say fantasy) of America as the holy nation. The doctrine, which has diverse origins in the American experience as a nation, is that America is a nation with a unique destiny, bestowed upon it by God.

This has had particularly vehement lip service in the Presidency of Ronald Reagan: in many instances he has pronounced America the embodiment of good, while America's presumed enemies, especially the Soviet Union, embody objective evil. Reagan thereby goes significantly beyond conventional or simplistic patriotic rhetoric. He is talking about imagined ultimate, cosmic confrontations.

Yet what is thus alleged about America's character as a nation and about the historic destiny of the nation has a curiously familar sound because it is, in fact, a bastard version of the biblical news about the election of Israel and then, in the New Testament, the vocation of the church as the exemplary nation or as the priest among the nations.

The appropriation of the biblical tradition concerning the holy nation for application to *any* secular regime, like the United States of America, is a profound affront at once to biblical faith and to the witness to the biblical events, as well as to the church of Christ. In an earlier time in the church's life, such an offense on the part of a ruler or incumbent official—like a president—might well have provoked the sanction of anathema. Do not suppose I am one bit facetious in considering that anathema should have been, in the present day, pronounced against President Reagan for his incessant trivialization of the Bible and its content. And he has no defense against anathema in a plea of sincerity. (There are, of course, many critics who label Reagan a hypocrite because he seldom darkens a church doorway. He used to say, when asked about his absences from church services, that his religion is too private a matter to warrant church attendance. That sounds sincere

enough to me, though it clearly places Reagan outside
the scope of biblical faith.) In any circumstance sincerity is no defense, and sincerity in denouncing and be-
littling the gospel only compounds the affront.
Reagan's entire well-worn story about America the holy
nation, America the divine favorite among the nations,
America the chosen nation is the rhetoric of fantasy, not
history; of delusion, not revelation; of gross vanity, not
fidelity or virtue. It is utterly anomalous—an outrage—
that Reagan should hear any applause for his rhetoric
or receive any adherents to his mythology about
America as the "justified" nation, particularly from any
constituency professing to be part of the church.

Understand, please, that I am not indulging here in
a partisan comment. And I do not single out Reagan in
a way that implies he is unique in his behavior and his
pontifical remarks in regard to the nation's moral disposition and its ultimate destiny. There are now, and
there have been for generations, Americans prominent
in the political establishment, rulers and authorities of
many partisan affiliations, in addition to ecclesiastical
leaders and officials and hosts of preachers, who have
mouthed various versions of this same fabrication about
America being an especially favored among nations by
God. The natural and diverse beauty of the continent
is taken to be a sign of that divine preference, and the
same idea is then translated into the grandiose dimensions of American technological prowess and military
superpower, or into "the American standard of living," or laissez-faire capitalism, or prosperity, or preeminence in science, and so on and on. The whole political discussion about maintaining America as
"Number 1" among the nations, which has, notably,

developed since the frustration of American super-power in Korea and then, grotesquely, in Vietnam, and subsequently in Lebanon and in Latin America, is part of this pathetic syndrome. The basic impression is that God has *so* favored America that God has rewarded America—by making and keeping the nation as "Number 1"—in advance of the Judgment.

That is only one of the ways in which this fantasizing about the nation works havoc (mainly in the form of mockery and ridicule) with biblical faith. For any professed church folk to be privy to these shibboleths about the nation is scandalous; for the president or adjacent high authorities to indulge and propagate the same is dangerous; for this credo to become widely accepted among the general citizenry borders on some sort of mass hallucination.

So Reagan is mentioned here by name because he has been an incumbent president and, in that capacity, has brought himself into the matter and extended the topic to greater extremities of rhetoric and myth than ever before. But, in naming him, we must keep in mind that there are legions more, among the American people and among those who purport to rule this society. Most sad to say, in these same ranks are multitudes of church-related folk, some hapless, some guileful, articulating these same themes.

I wish this whole matter were innocuous, just an irritation occasioned by careless and excessive language, a mere distortion of some elements of America's past, an issue of "civic religion," which, though intellectually corrupt and bankrupt in terms of spirituality, is unlikely to disrupt society in a practical manner. But this is not an innocuous cause; it is one both pernicious and perilous for society and one rapidly become a crisis.

I do not give much credence to conspiratorial interpretations of history, but I apprehend that the truth is that there are persons and organizations and financing resources seeking to transmute the mythology and rhetoric concerning America the holy nation into a political and ideological movement to "convert" America into a so-called Christian nation. Some of these powers speak of restoring America as a "Christian nation"—in blatant falsification of American history as well as remarkable distortion of what it means, in biblical perspective, to be Christian. The stridency of Mr. Reagan's exclamations concerning the nation's peculiar, divine-oriented destiny feeds the extraordinary goal which these certain principalities and persons intend to attain. Their determination already is sufficient to rationalize the purging (I use the term literally) of those who stand in their way, whether the latter be from the churches or the traditional political parties or the media or among incumbent officeholders or assorted non-Christian minorities. I conclude that such forces actually gather; they meet, they strategize, they launch pilot exercises, they recruit support, they get ready for their own style coup d'état. Meanwhile, they manipulate Reagan and others who have power or influence temporarily, and they largely dominate and direct a vast, unfortunate, misled constituency—generally assembled as the "Moral Majority"—who have become ripe for such exploitation because of their long experience of economic, cultural, and political rejection in America. They are enough disillusioned that they are no longer willing to abide waiting for recognition and for their share of *everything* until the Kingdom comes. They have always been impatient for *that*, and now the promise of *something* for them in "the Christian nation" (if not in the Eschaton) is a promise they have nothing to lose in embracing. And, it must be acknowledged, those who are doing the exploiting of the hapless multitude are very skillful and ambitious hucksters indeed.

This cause of the so-called Christian nation has already accomplished notable successes politically, particularly in its vendettas against certain legislators, in its surveillance network, in locating and committing huge funding, and in its preliminary agenda of "family" laws: its oppression—sometimes of hysterical scope—of homosexuals and its assault upon the First Amendment, its disruption of the free library system, its interference with school administrations and curriculum policies, and its efforts to legislate morality in the narrowest construction of that term. In 1984, Mr. Reagan, a presidential candidate for reelection (in manifest need of some public distraction from his failures in foreign policy, his dispatching of marines to their doom, the multifarious mundane corruptions of his highest-level appointees, and his callous rejection of the poor and dispossessed and aged and handicapped and ill and unemployed and unemployable), by pushing the snarled school prayer issue to the forefront, has given those seeking to found or restore "a Christian nation" in America a large opportunity to pursue their aims under cover of the school prayer debate.

The school prayer controversy is one of those debilitating public disputes that is mostly sham and not substance, the sort of conflict which conceals other issues that seldom openly surface and thus are infrequently ei-

ther honestly faced or appropriately settled. It is, therefore, a situation with many possibilities for distraction
or diversion and with a multitude of opportunities for
manipulation for covert purposes. The literal public debate in the school prayer issue has a strong resem-
blance to an exchange of cursings instead of an informed dialogue about policy alternatives. And the
prayer controversy has been a virtually classic example
of the substitution of a public relations campaign for de-
liberative policy-making. It is, in other words, not only
the case that we have been diverted from Central
America and what is happening there by indulgence in
the public arguments about school prayer, but within
the context of those arguments there has been little of
a substantive character and very much sound and fury.

Consider the repeated one-liner, used by advocates
of prayer in the schools, including Ronald Reagan, to
the effect that the Supreme Court in its Constitutional
bar to school prayer had "expelled God from school."
This is patently absurd talk, Constitutionally irrelevant
and, perhaps more significant, an open ridicule of God.
It does not, in the first place, speak of the living God at
all but of some notion or conception of "God"—a puny
one, at that—the location or other reference to which is
dependent upon the actions of human beings, or of
some humans and institutions. The Supreme Court, the
school board, a teacher, or whoever is to determine, according to this profane remark, where "God" is and, indeed, what (what, not who, is the correct term here)
God is thought to be. I believe that such a comment,
and the view of deity it conceals, may be offensive to
many persons and communities, but whatever the circumstance with others, it is radically objectionable to

biblical faith and to the community of the church of Christ. From a biblical point of view, there is nothing whatever that the Supreme Court or any school board or any principalities or any persons—including any President of the United States—can say or do that can determine the character or action of the Word of God in common history—and nothing, issuing from any such source, that can obviate, diminish, alter, modify, prejudice, detract from, or otherwise change the pervasive presence of the Word of God in this world. For Christians, when it is said the court decision has "expelled God from school," the speaker is both denouncing and denying the presence of the Word of God everywhere in this world or, what is also conceivable, the one speaking is supercilious and ignorant and simply does not know what he or she is talking about.

By the same token, the access of a human being, including students and teachers, to the Word of God is in no way curtailed or lessened or estopped or rendered any more difficult by the decision made by the Supreme Court. Nor has prayer been inhibited in any manner whatsoever. In fact, as one would expect, those who complain that "God" has been lately expelled from school are for the most part incapable of enunciating in comprehensible language and syntax what is the reality of the relationship of prayer. One ends up with some plaintive exercises—nonprayers or antiprayers addressed to some nongod or antigod. Better that the children spend a few moments at the opening of the school day meditating on the meaning of the Constitutional amendments that comprise the Bill of Rights: Let them be spared the foolish indignity of making believe they are praying to a make-believe deity conjured up in a White House press handout.

The Necessity of Repentance

Biblical spirituality is not expressed in goals and agendas, regimens and attainments; it is not concerned in any degree with any effort to earn justification. Those who expend themselves in accordance with some scheme which bears a label of spirituality in order to try to prove or verify their moral worth are in reality attempting to second-guess how they are and will be judged in the Word of God at the ending of the history of the present age. That attempt can avail nothing whatever. The Judgment of the Word of God—both in its general character as the consummation of history and also in its particularity, whereby every thought, word, deed, and omission of every person and every principality from the commencement of time remain secret as the very Word of God until uttered. There is no foresight available to either institutions or humans which has the integrity to forecast the tenor of the Judgment as an event or the substance of the Judgment with respect to any creature or any decision or act of any creature. So far as human beings are concerned, such anxieties concerning justification or attempts to anticipate how the Word of God judges this or that exceed the actual capabilities of humans. Hence the very effort to second-guess the Judgment must be counted as a dehumanization of persons which is very radical and very fearsome. Part of the reality of what happens in such circumstances is, paradoxically, not a projection of the

Judgment which is coming but a recapitulation of the
primal issue between humankind and creation and the
Word of God, which, in traditional biblical insight, occasions the fall and the consignment of the whole of
creation to the power of death. That issue concerns a
vanity which belittles God and the office of God. Repentance of that initiates biblical spirituality.

Are human beings, then, just hapless victims of the
fall awaiting the secret Judgment of the Word of God
at the end of the era? By no means. To affirm that humans (and principalities, for that matter) are incapable
of acting to justify themselves as they are also incapaci-
tated from sanctifying themselves simply means, on
one hand, that the work of redemption in fallen creation is entirely and aptly the vocation of the Word of
God in this world, and that the human and corporate
recognition of that truth is essentially a matter of confession and repentance. The content or message of such
confession and repentance is the radical acknowledge-
ment of helplessness. As it has been put before, if you
want to know what you can do to justify yourself, the
biblical response is: You must give up trying to justify
yourself and confess your utter helplessness in the face
of the power of death. This repentance is the substance
of biblical spirituality. *Utter* helplessness is what is involved, without any equivocation or qualification or
deferral or caveat or double-talk. The repentance at
issue is such that it apprehends the empirical risk of
death or of abandonment; that is, the risk that there is
no Word of God to identify you and give you your
name. Without that gift of your name, you do not exist; you are dead or, as they say, as good as dead.

As it is for persons, so it is for the principalities and

powers, the nations and institutions, the regimes, systems, authorities, bureaucracies, causes, organizations, ideologies, classes, and similar realms. It has, after all, been evident since the vocation of John the Baptist—and, in the Old Testament, since the witness of Isaiah—that repentance and the confession of the vitality of the Word of God are not merely personal or private matters but are notoriously public and blatantly political.

The problem of America as a nation, in biblical perspective, remains this elementary issue of repentance. The United States is, as all nations are, called in the Word of God to repentance. That, in truth, is what the church calls for, whether knowingly or not, every time the church prays *Thy Kingdom come.*

America needs to repent. Every episode in the common experience of America as a nation betells that need. If such be manifest in times of trauma and trouble—such as now—it is as much the need in triumphal or grandiose circumstances.

The nation needs to repent. If I put the matter so baldly, I hope no one will mistake my meaning for the rhetoric of those electronic celebrity preachers who sometimes use similar language to deplore the mundane lusts of the streets or the ordinary vices of people or to berate the Constitutional bar to prayer, so-called, in public schools while practicing quietism about the genocidal implications of the Pentagon's war commerce or extolling indifference toward the plight of the swelling urban underclasses.

Topically, repentance is *not* about forswearing wickedness as such; repentance concerns the confession of vanity. For America—for any nation at any time—*repentance means confessing blasphemy.*

Blasphemy occurs in the existence and conduct of a nation whenever there is such profound and sustained confusion as to the nation's character, place, capabilities, and destiny that the vocation of the Word of God is preempted or usurped. Thus the very presumption of the righteousness of the American cause as a nation *is* blasphemy.

Americans, for some time now, have been assured, again and again, that the United States will prevail in history because the American cause is righteous. Anyone who believes that has, to say the very least, learned nothing from the American adventurism in Vietnam. Then, a succession of presidents made similar pronouncements, but America suffered ignominious defeat nonetheless. And if in the last few years some sense of guilt about Vietnam has begun to surface, this has been, for the most part, a strange and perverted sentiment because it has attached not to the crimes of American intervention in Southeast Asia—to massacre, despoilment, and genocide—but to the event of American defeat. To feel guilty because America lost, rather than because of what America did, is another, if macabre, instance of false righteousness. That is only the more underscored when the unlawful invasion of Grenada is examined as an attempt to fantasize the victory for American superpower which was missed in Vietnam.

Furthermore, the confusion of a nation's destiny, and of a nation's capabilities, with the vocation of the Word of God in history—which is the *esse* of blasphemy—sponsors the delusion that America exercises domination over creation as well as history and that it can and should control events in the life of creation. Other nations, ancient and modern, as has been mentioned, suffer similar delusions, but if there ever has been a nation which should know better (that is, which should repent), it is America, if only because of the American experience as a nation and a society in these past few decades.

After all, it is only in the period since, say, Hiroshima, in which American power, rampant most conspicuously in the immense, redundant, overkill nuclear-weapons arsenal, has been proven impotent, because if it is deployed, it portends self-destruction, and if it is not, it amounts to profligate, grotesque waste. In either instance, American nuclear arms are rendered practically ineffectual in dominating events, but they still mock the sovereignty of the Word of God in history.

Much the same must, of course, be said of the nation's society and culture, which has become, as I have earlier remarked, overdependent upon the consumption ethic, with its doctrines of indiscriminate growth, gross development, greedy exploitation of basic resources, uncritical and often stupid reliance upon technological capabilities and incredible naiveté about technological competence, and crude, relentless manipulation of human beings as consumers. Increasingly, now, people can glimpse that this is no progress, no enhancement of human life, but wanton plunder of creation itself. People begin to apprehend that the penultimate implementation of the American consumption ethic is, bluntly, self-consumption. In the process, it has become evident as well that the commerce engendered by the American consumption ethic, together with the commerce of weapons proliferation, relates consequentially to virtually every injustice of which human beings are victims in this nation and in much of the rest of the world.

And so I say the United States needs to repent; the nation needs to be freed of blasphemy. These are, admittedly, theological statements. Yet I think they are also truly practical statements. America will remain frustrated, literally demoralized, incapable of coping with its concrete problems as a nation and society until it knows that realism concerning the nation's vocation which only repentance can bring.

One hopes repentance will be forthcoming. If not, it *will* happen: in the good time of the Judgment of the Word of God.

Meanwhile, in this same context, persons repent and all persons are called to repentance. The confession and repentance of an individual does not take place, as some preachers and the like aver, in a great void, abstracted from the everyday existence of this world. The experience of each penitent is peculiar to that person, but that does not mean it is separated from the rest of created life.

This is the reason why the foisting of any stereotype of the experience upon people is coercive and false and, indeed, self-contradictory. It must be recognized, however, that this is quite what is involved where, for an example, a so-called born-again Christian stereotype is asserted. I can testify personally that I have been "born again"—my account constitutes the book aptly titled *A Second Birthday*—but that appears to mean something substantively different from sudden, momentary trauma. I do not thus imply that the latter is invalid or necessarily incomplete or otherwise questionable, but I do question the composition of *any* stereotype of the experience and the insinuation that it is normative, much less mandatory.

What is implicated in confession and repentance, which inaugurates the practice of a biblical spirituality whatever the style or detail of what happens to a particular person, is the establishment or restoral by the Word of God of that person's identity in the Word of God in a way in which the query *Who am I?* merges with the question *Where is God?* The transaction comprehends, as has been said, the risk that there is no one or nothing to affirm a person's existence and identity. As I have put it before, the confession of utter helplessness, the repentance which is requisite and efficacious, always involves the empirical risk of death. At the very same time, this repentance foreshadows and anticipates the perfection of each person's and each principality's vocation in the Kingdom of God.

Justification and Hope

Since the disillusionment and defection of Judas, a recurrent issue for people of biblical faith has been the confusion between justification and justice. It is, in fact, out of contemporary manifestations of that very confusion, especially during the decade of the sixties, that many Christian activists (as the media style them) have become more curious about spirituality and have begun to explore the significance of biblical spirituality for political decisions and actions. The widespread posthumous interest in the witness and ministry of Thomas Merton is one significant sign of that, as I have said.

I do not venture to unravel the confusion regarding justification and justice in terms of its prolonged and agitated annals in Christendom. I speak of the matter only theologically, not historically and analytically. As I understand it, justice is the accomplishment of the Judgment of the Word of God in the consummation of this age and embodies all the specifications, all the particular details of the Judgment with respect to all things whatsoever. Justice, as it is articulate in the Judgment, is essentially an expression of the faithfulness of the Word of God to the creation of the Word of God.

There is no capability in human effort or in the enterprise of nations or other principalities to approximate the justice of the Judgment. The decisions and actions of persons and powers may, in a sense, aspire to or render tribute to the justice of the Judgment, but they cannot fabricate it or duplicate it or preempt it. And, as has been mentioned, when they suppose that they have in given circumstances imitated or second-guessed the Judgment and its justice, they are most in jeopardy so far as the integrity of their respective vocations is concerned. Persons and principalities can neither play God nor displace God without risking self-destruction. This does not denigrate at all the struggle for justice in merely human and institutional terms; in fact, it upholds that struggle even in recognizing how fragile, transient, and ambiguous it is—and dynamic—how open it is to amendment, how vulnerable to change.

Within the scene of this world, now, where the struggle for justice in merely human and institutional translations is happening, and in the midst of the turmoil that stirs, the Word of God, as a matter of God's own prerogative, freedom, and grace, offers the assurance of redemption, the promise of wholeness and integrity and communication, the message of hope in the Kingdom which is to come together with the Judgment of the Word of God and the justice which that Judgment works.

This justification is both credible and accessible, not because any person, or any society, is worthy but because the Word of God is extravagant or, if you will, because the *Word of God is godly*. So the grace of the Word of God transcends the injustice of the present age, agitates the resilience of those who struggle now to expose and rebuke injustice, informs those who resist the rulers of the prevailing darkness, and overflows in eagerness for the coming of One who is the Judge of this world and whose justice reigns forevermore. By virtue of justification, we are freed now to live in hope.

CHAPTER THREE

HOPE AND JUDGMENT

The righteous will rejoice when he sees the
    vengeance;
  he will bathe his feet in the blood of the
    wicked.
Men will say, "Surely there is a reward for the
    righteous;
  surely there is a God who judges on earth."
                                        Psalm 58

It has lately come to pass that America has entered upon a dark age. This is, I discern, also the reality for other postindustrial technocratic societies. It is, I believe, an authentic dark age; that is, a time in which the power of death is pervasive and militant and in which people exist without hope or else in pursuit of transient, fraudulent, or delusive hopes. It is not merely an episode of passing malaise, nor only an interlude of economic or cultural or political depression, though it has some such aspects. It is an era of chaotic activity, disoriented priorities, banal redundancy. Creativity is suppressed; imagination has been lost; nostalgia is superficial and indulgent. Society suffers massive tedium. There is very quick resort to violence, usually of overkill dimensions. People become frantic about their personal safety and concentrate solemnly on their own survival. The infrastructures of great institutions crumble. For those who consider that there is a God, there is widespread suspicion of abandonment. It is a period marked by intense animosity toward human life and, indeed, intransigent hostility toward all of created life. It is a time within itself persuasive of the truth of the biblical description of the fall. It is a prosperous period for death. It is, in short, a dark age.

A Dark Age

That the contemporary phase of American experience may be characterized as verifying the fall does not mean that this dark age is severed from history. On the contrary, it was incipient in the Second World War and foreshadowed in the supposed ending of that war in the resort to obliteration bombing and, next, the deployment of first-strike nuclear weapons against Hiroshima and Nagasaki. It was then that the primal features of the present darkness began to emerge and became capable of being identified.

A rudimentary element in this time is violence, and not as a last resort but as the first reliance of the nation and society, and then not only externally in confronting other nations as enemies but also internally in the paramilitarization of police power and its entanglement with the entrenchment of racism. Moreover, it is not only visible violence—as in nuclear arms or paramilitary police operations—which is involved, but, as much, invisible violence, like that practiced in the discard of the elderly, or that which is often routinely administered in the medical and hospital systems. America is a violent society not because there are not viable alternatives to violence but because, in the Second World War and in the so-called cold war, violence has been the first, quick, and often preemptive recourse in substitution for the policy or the practice of nonviolence. The nation learned the techniks of violence and handled the varieties of violence in these war encounters and fantasies and also became entrapped into supposing that violence is good. Thus a literally fatal idolatry of violence has been initiated.

Another hallmark of this dark age is, manifestly, technology and the political implementation of technology as technocracy. This was foreseeable, the Second World War and the cold war aside, but it is a syndrome which has been enormously influenced by the war events. This is the realm in which America has most self-consciously imitated and emulated the Nazis and, indeed, vested former Nazis with employment, with great power, with handsome compensation and similar rewards, and with limitless facilities to abet the momentum of the technological process. The central issue in technology has been and still is the proposition that any technological capability which develops should be implemented without restraint of human discretion as to whether a particular capability has a potential adverse to human life or to the life of creation. This is the unbridled amoral technology that has yielded a proliferation of harmful, stupid, unneeded consumer products as well as nuclear weapons and, for that matter, nuclear utilities.

At the same time, as an additional feature of the American darkness, forms of technology have enabled the articulation of conditioning, marketing, and merchandising techniks capable of utterly overpowering human faculties of reason or conscience, of neutralizing human critical responses, and of programming more or less everyone to purchase and consume whatever technology produces. Applied politically as well as commercially, similar techniks have had a devastating impact upon the fiber of democratic institutions by minimizing intelligent citizen participation and in substituting image for substance, polling for voting, and credibility for truth. What is at issue in politics, as in the marketplace, as Mr. Nixon demonstrated so convincingly, is not truth or falsehood in a factual sense (much less metaphysically) but that which human beings can be induced, in one way or another, to believe whether or not it is connected to the truth. In this process, which is central in the politicalization of technology, language is warped, inverted, and eventually destroyed for the purposes of human communication or human direction of institutions; instead, human beings become robots, reacting reflexively to sound signals to which they have been programmed. Sometimes this extraordinary change in human beings, which is happening now in the American technocratic state, is referred to under the nomenclature of "computer literacy," but it is really a synonym for death.

An Idolatry of Science

The present darkness in America has complicated origins in diverse aspects of the American experience as a culture and society—compounded, as has already been mentioned in setting forth some features of the age, by certain historic events. Perhaps the most conspicuous cultural factor has been a profligate idolatry of science, fostering gross overestimations of the capabilities of science and technology, together with an uncritical—indeed, wanton—imposition of the scientific method, so-called, throughout society. These circumstances have, in turn, issued in the literally fantastic attitude that technical capability ought to be implemented just because it exists, without regard to the moral character of any particular venture. Views such as these are embraced in a belief, inculcated profusely in the culture, that science is morally neutral or, to put it in some traditional theological terms, that science as a principality somehow enjoys exemption from the fall. This naiveté, incredible though it be, is commonly associated with the rank superstition that science can eventually supply a remedy for any peril or problem wrought from the untimely, stupid, or inappropriate implementation of any specific technical capability.

The practical consequences of these foolish verities have been multifarious, nefarious, and, often enough, grotesque. Thus, to mention but a single item, hundreds of thousands of hapless Americans today await tardy rescue from hazards unprojected or, anyway, unforewarned by commercialized science, fomented by reckless, premature, or otherwise improvident disposal of toxic wastes.

In Hiroshima (which is simultaneously the primeval and the penultimate event of nuclear history), such ideas sponsored within the pantheon of science converged with the shibboleths spawned initially during the Second World War, which were readily enough extended and embellished to suit the cold war and which survive still, in substantially this latter form, in the Pentagon, in the so-called intelligence apparatus, and among the self-styled national security authorities. The upshot has been the much-boasted connection between zeal for American nuclear preeminence and that fancied holy destiny for the nation in postwar America, along with the asserted efficacy of superpower in determining history and in dominating the life of creation, not to mention the extraordinary, if nonetheless self-evident, contradiction of the doctrine of nuclear deterrence.

Events have, by now, intervened and surpassed the heavy myths originating in Hiroshima: American nuclear preeminence has been dissipated and, perchance, was all along illusory. The inherent impotence of superpower to feign sovereignty in history and domination over the existence of creation has been verified in one calamity after another befalling the professed superpowers (such has been the repeated lesson in Korea, Vietnam, Afghanistan, Poland, and Central America). At the same time, the doctrine of deterrence seems discredited by the common sense of the ordinary citizen.

Meanwhile, the fundamental proposition which rendered the making and use of nuclear weapons thinkable in the first place—the curious hypothesis that science is morally innocuous or morally neutral—continues to be categorically refuted, day after day, not only because of the close probabilities of nuclear apocalypse but also because of the plethora of other perils and contaminations, plagues and pestilences, and jeopardies both known and surprise, produced and promoted in the name of science as safe and beneficial to life.

In short, in the present time in America—and, indeed, on this planet—history itself confirms the radical and persistent moral ambiguity of science and of all that science does and claims: History verifies and betells the truth that science is a fallen principality.

An Assault Upon Sanity and Conscience

The extraordinary changes being wrought in American society by the politicalization of technology are not only literally counterrevolutionary in scope in their impact upon the inherited Constitutional tradition but, further, represent a massive and sustained aggression against human beings and the faculties most definitive of human life. What is going on is a brutal assault upon sanity and conscience. The reality is that technology and its political formulation as technocracy cannot prevail and, most especially, cannot secure its totalitarian captivation of the nation unless—somehow—human beings are dissuaded from functioning humanly. Technocracy requires the displacement of human creativity and the neutralization of human reason by intimidation, the inducement of ignorance, passivity, indifference, indolence, diversion, coercion, or some other form of dysfunction. The process is, as often as not, abetted simply by neglect or default or acquiescence on the part of persons.

Technocracy requires this abdication or equivalent loss of human originality and reflection in order to achieve a maximum efficiency, as gauged by its own terms. The human involvement must therefore, so far as possible, be reduced to that which is quantifiable, predictable, reliable, uniform, and, in a word, conformed to the survival interests of the technocracy rather than concerned with human potential, human rights, or human needs.

The requirement which technocracy has to neutralize human discretion, particularly where that openly identifies moral problems, explains for the most part why the last two decades have been marked with such emphatic, at times virtually pathological, anxiety about so-called security, surveillance, the tracking of credit histories and political involvements, and the great inflation of the police presence in society, while at the same time civilian control of the police has been practically set aside.

Meanwhile, the capability of technology to displace human activities by substituting ersatz technical procedures steadily increases and encroaches upon human responsibility. "Knowledge engineering," whereby a computer classifies and applies prefabricated "solutions" to societal problems, is ominous in its potential for eliminating human reason and conscience from social crisis. Similar schemas are already in wide use in medicine and, increasingly, in law, as well as in the media, with, so far as I can discern, appalling consequences for human life in society. One of the perils in this kind of substitution and displacement, as is happening so rapidly with respect to language, for an example, is that the substitute is readily confused with the authentic, and after a while the genuine disappears because of neglect or disuse and all that is left is the ersatz and some further diminished human beings.

In my household, for instance, the custom is to use oranges, when they are available, in order to squeeze juice from them. Orange juice, made in that way, is in every respect superior to juice "reconstituted." I have never had synthetic juice. However, a guest in the household, a younger person, sometime ago complained to me when served genuine orange juice squeezed from real oranges. The guest declared that Tang—a wholly synthetic product composed chiefly of chemicals—would have been preferred. For this guest, I believe, the ersatz had replaced the authentic and the fake product was in fact regarded as if it were the real thing. The incident is seemingly minor—but the same kind of change is happening *everywhere* in America, and it has transmuted the quality of life for human beings to a radical degree while also occasioning the preemption of human capabilities of thought and response. This process of substitution and displacement is a principal manner in which political and cultural conformity is reached. It is no less insidious because it is, so to say, invisible or because it does not resort to overt coercion.

One very important accompaniment of the displacement process and the human dysfunction that it prompts, in one way or another, is the manifold increase in the theatrical and ritual aspects of the governing institutions, both nominal and actual. The most poignant instance of this affects the Presidency. In the urgency of the Second World War, the Presidency lost much of its effectiveness as a ruling authority to other and extra-Constitutional agencies and institutions, notably the Pentagon. Instead of the control and direction of the Pentagon lodging in the Presidency, the Presidency became subject to the initiative, briefing, indoctrination, and dominance of the Pentagon. After the war had ostensibly ended, this reversal of roles continued and became more complex, more institutionalized or routine, as compared to the relatively extemporaneous status that it had had during wartime. For one thing, the budget-making procedure, which is always also basic policy-making, became extended, for the sake of longer-range contingency planning, so that the Pentagon was projecting budget (and policy) years ahead of the fiscal constructions of the president or the Congress. To a substantial extent, those projections became presumptions or otherwise gained priority in the budgets adopted. In this change, however, the scope of the president was diminished. The president, together with the Congress, was much more in the position of ratifying the Pentagon's budget (and policy) than of originating budget and policy. That represents a stereotypical problem in relation to any bureaucracy, but it is an acute issue, and one adversely affecting the whole Constitutional system and its values wherein they are weighted on the side of human life, in the technocratic regime. Other factors aggravate the situation, including the tradition of presidential accountability in elections every four years. The Pentagon technocracy cannot tolerate these disruptions, and so it is deemed best to relocate the Presidency as far as possible outside the mainstream of policy deliberation and decision and to take on the chore of indoctrinating each incumbent president now and then in what is going on or what is contemplated and what he can appropriately say and do.

In other words, the Presidency is cast more and more in a ritual or theatrical aspect, in which the pretense is upheld that the president governs while the president, if well behaved, is in fact engaged in diverting attention from the realpolitik of the nation. When citizens ask rhetorically, *What difference does it make who is elected president?* the answer is not that all the candidates are the same in qualification or lack of it, because they vary significantly in these respects, as well as ethically and aesthetically. Rather, the response is, *It doesn't make much difference,* because the Presidency is no longer the primary governing institution in America. So it is not ironical or absurd, in a day when the Presidency has been reduced to ceremonial and public relations and other theatrical assignments, to elect a professional actor to the office.

Notice, please, that I do not allege that this erosion of Constitutional authority in favor of Pentagon technocracy has been happening because of wicked persons in high places in that technocracy. There are, no doubt, truly wicked persons there, as one would expect in any such vast enterprise, but that is not the problem I am raising here. On the contrary, the Pentagon institutional apparatus is basically organized for the mere sake of the survival of the institution *regardless* of the character or disposition of any human beings within the precincts of the technocracy. The Pentagon is instituted to maximize its likelihood of survival no matter who the people are who nominally lead or direct it and no matter who the rank-and-file personnel may be. What irony there is in the institutional operation is that which arises from the assertion (standard in Pentagon press releases) that this array of anonymous and conformed staff members represents a professional cadre possessing expertise. The latter assertion, of course, is really only a defensive posture, intended to protect the vested interests of the personnel in the technocracy's surviving indefinitely in its present shape; it is one which has nothing to do with knowledge, skill, competence, honesty, or accountability.

I do not dwell on the Pentagon as an example of some of the conflicts between a technocratic regime and human life, or of the irreconcilability between technocracy and the constitutional tradition, because the Pentagon is institutionally unique. On the contrary, I do so because the Pentagon is archetypical of the principalities and powers of the technocratic state and is representative in its operation of how any of the great public or private corporate powers act and of how they victimize human beings, not only ordinary folk but presidents or others in high office too. I am aware, let it be mentioned, that these comments about how the principalities function for their own survival in the technocratic regime is very simplified, and I recognize that the reality of their scene is more complex than human language can explicate briefly; indeed, the scene is literally chaos, the chaos of death's own reign.

For all that, let it be acknowledged that the principalities of technocracy cannot calculate failure. They must succeed or be able, on some basis, to declare that they succeed. That is why, in part, the disastrous defeat of American superpower in Southeast Asia could not be tolerated by the Pentagon. And when a whole battery of public relations campaigns still did not dispose of the truth, something else had to be attempted. A rehearsal was staged, macabre as it was, when the Iranian hostages were released (after the air rescue operation, which was macabre too, was estopped). That tried to construe the release as some sort of victory, and it was dutifully celebrated as such when the hostages arrived home. We had, however, to await a different president to witness a real war in which American aggression in an unlawful invasion became victorious to supply vicariously what had not been won in Vietnam. Grenada thus was the Pentagon's way of bringing Vietnam to a glorious and patriotic finish. I suppose many, many Americans in addition to the Pentagon cadre and the President have been so stifled and conformed that they are fooled by this grotesque trick, which assumes that Americans are, by now, bereft of either sanity or conscience.

A Monastic Witness

Vietnam manifestly still haunts the nation; the Pentagon has no power (indeed, no authority) to exorcise that ghastly, searing, deadly recollection. That was pathetically attested lately in the misadventure of the dispatch of marines to Lebanon. Fantasy and war have—I suppose—always had close associations, but if that be so, the two have seldom become so jumbled each with the other as in that incomprehensible assignment in Lebanon. One gathers that, in fantasy, it was supposed to be a heroic episode that would serve the purpose of repressing further the still vivid recall of the humiliation of American superpower in Vietnam. And, even though Lebanon was, on its own scale, an equivalent calamity for American superpower, the temptations for other exploits riddle the situations in the Middle East and also in Central America. Those temptations are likely to insinuate themselves against America for a long time to come—if, that is, the world is spared nuclear war and there *is* a long time to come.

If the assessment of the ruling powers in the American technocratic state expressed here is accurate to any substantial degree, then resistance is warranted: a patient, resilient, versatile, tough-minded resistance to the powers that be, urgently needed among all persons who still remember the Constitutional inheritance and, especially, the Bill of Rights, and all those who would prefer representative government over a secret, unaccountable, anonymous, self-perpetuating technocratic totalitarianism. Or, on a broader basis, such resistance is called for as both an exemplification and a defense of human life in society as such.

For Christians, of course, participation in such resistance to the ruling authorities because the purported ruling authorities operate on an arbitrary basis, without means of accountability to human beings and to human life, is, theologically speaking, normative. It has been since the days of the apostles an articulation of the characteristic and indispensable confession of the political efficacy of the resurrection from death.

There began to emerge from the civil rights movement and the antiwar protests, in the sixties, a confessing movement, ecumenical in character and constituency, powerless in the world connotations of power, extemporaneous in its political actions, biblical in its claims to authority and credibility, strongly reminiscent of the anti-Nazi resistance. That coalition has become concentrated now particularly in the antinuclear effort, and if it lacks the organic cohesion for which some (not myself) yearn, it is still coherent enough to exercise the very definitive human faculties which are being atrophied by the routine of the technocratic regime. After all, if the technocratic principalities and powers are engaged in a prodigious and detailed assault upon human sanity and conscience, the most essential and wise resistance involves using those faculties which are endangered.

Despite the pervasive propaganda about criminality in contemporary America, it remains the case that large numbers of prisoners in this country are, in truth, political prisoners. Their common offense against the powers that command the means of arrest, prosecution, conviction, and imprisonment has been their recalcitrance to conformity; they have practiced sanity and conscience.

Those whose political nonconformity occasions their status as political prisoners are, from the viewpoint of the ruling authorities, eliminated by being confined. The same remedy, with some few aesthetic amendments, is often deployed against others who remain unconformed or who are simply deemed useless—such as the retarded, the disabled, the elderly, the retired, children in certain instances, the poor, the unemployable, the homeless. The confinement of society's outcasts or surplus people, though a considerable expense, can take many and adaptive forms and has the great advantage, so far as the rulers are concerned, of rendering them more or less invisible.

Technocracy must be resisted, and human beings must reclaim discretion over every facet of technology and every possible implementation of technical capacity. For biblical people, the claim goes further: Technology and technical capability must be rendered accountable to human life and to the sovereignty of the Word of God, in whom all things, including science and technology, and all of life, including that of the principalities and nations, have been created. In other words, the authority which Christians assert when they engage in resistance to the incumbent technocratic regime is their confession that Jesus Christ is Lord or that the sovereignty of the Word of God in history is active *now*.

Whatever other forms that witness of resistance may take, I believe it must incorporate two aspects of venerable monastic tactics, which also have origins in biblical spirituality. The first of these is intercession—the *work* of intercession and, if you will, the *politics* of intercession—the solemn offering to Almighty God of all the cares and needs of this world whatsoever represented in the offertory of certain particular necessities and issues implicating persons and communities known to those who intercede. In the tradition of intercession, as I understand it, the one who intercedes for another is confessing that his or her trust in the vitality of the Word of God is so serious that he or she volunteers risks sharing the burden of the one for whom intercession is offered even to the extremity of taking the place of the other person who is the subject of the prayer. Intercession takes its meaning from the politics of redemption. Intercession is a most audacious witness to the world.

Another aspect of the monastic style I consider especially suited to political resistance is sustained eucharistic praise of the Word of God. In the Bible, in such images or stories as we have received concerning the Kingdom of God, the only activity which seems pertinent in the Kingdom (including those scenes of the Judgment that are integral to the coming of the Kingdom) is praise of the Word of God. It is as if the vocations of the whole assembly of created life, the angelic powers as well as human beings and the entire remainder and range of creation, are being fulfilled and perfected in celebration of the Word of God, in the glorification of the Word of God, in thanksgiving for the Word of God. For human beings, in these scenes, it is not God who is fulfilled or made whole by the praise but we ourselves.

This effort of the chorus of creation in the Kingdom is the consummation of the restoration of creation wrought by the Word of God. That restoration has begun in the midst of the fall; it has been exemplified in Jesus Christ (and so we name him *Lord*); our witness *now* expects, eagerly, and anticipates, patiently, the Kingdom vouchsafed at the finale of the present history and at the end of time. Hence the occasion for praising the Word of God, in every way, in all things, is already with us. There is actually nothing else that needs to be done, and so whatever we do is transfigured into a sacrament of that praise.

IN THE MATTER OF MORTIFICATION OF THE FLESH

*Let not those who hope in thee be put to shame
    through me,
  O Lord GOD of hosts;
Let not those who seek thee be brought to
    dishonor through me,
  O God of Israel.*

                                        Psalm 69

As I was saying at the outset, in the time in which I have been writing this book on what I understand to be spirituality with precedent and authority in the biblical witness, I have been much afflicted with pain.

Diagnostically, the trouble happens in my legs, where, because of the toll of advanced diabetes, the arterial circulation is sorely obstructed. It is the third time in my life when amputation of these limbs has become a serious threat, and, with the help offered in chelation therapy, I struggle against that outcome. I am at once fatigued and bored with this recurring effort and I consider giving it up. But then it comes to mind how eagerly death has pursued me, in ways that have made me self-conscious, and then I become angry toward death and defiant. I suppose there is some spite toward death involved; in any case, my outrage seems to enhance my stamina. So I resist. I resist the power of death and that which, in the somewhat pathetic state of my health, manifestly foreshadows death—like amputation of a leg or two.

So there is pain. In the present episode there is virtually no respite from pain because I have refused chemicals as "pain relievers." I have (I will not burden you with an elaborate argument here) become convinced that such medications are more harmful to me than anything else that can be said for them. I do not consider my abstinence either brave or foolish; it is simply a circumstance typical of those which occur in fallen existence.

Pain is not a stranger in my life (nor, really, in anybody else's life), and I am familiar with some of the temptations that attend pain. That is one of the subjects of the book *A Second Birthday*, and of course I have been recalling those commentaries lately. I know, for instance, how preemptive pain can be—excluding practically everything and everyone else from its victim's intelligence or consideration. Or I realize how pain agitates vanity and, most specifically, sponsors a false sense of being justified by suffering. So from the outset of the current affliction, I have had, from past experience, some insight, beyond gritting my teeth, into coping with the reality of pain and with some of the subtleties of pain. And while there have been moments when I have cried out, I do not think that I have been brutalized by what has been taking place, and I do not consider that I have been demoralized either.

Still, in the circumstances, I am haunted by questions: *Why is this happening to me?* and *Why is it happen-*

ing now? Or, *Is this some cruel or perverse accounting for my past sins and oversights?* And, *If I forebear to blame myself for my pain, who is left to blame but God?* Again, *Is my suffering of pain consequentially related to the massive default and multiple failures of commercialized medicine? Is pain, thus, an injustice? And in its essence more an issue of politics than of medical practice?* On the other hand, *Can this endurance of pain somehow be edifying? How is it related to the gospel?*

I just begin the roster of queries, I do not exhaust the list. I also have no settled answers to any of these questions (some of which truly rank as conundrums). I just live with such issues, as I live with the pain. And I trust the Word of God until the latter day, when all of created life, myself included, gather at the throne of the Judgment of this world and when the disposition of all these questions and that of all questions whatsoever shall become notorious. *Lord, have mercy upon us; Christ, have mercy upon us; Lord, have mercy upon us.*

Meanwhile we are all called to live by grace—that is, concretely—to live in a way (even in pain) which trusts the Judgment of the Word of God in history. I realize that some who are reading this book, if they have persevered to this page, would have preferred a book on "spirituality" which pronounced some rules, some norms, some guidelines, some rubrics for a sacred discipline that, if pursued diligently, would establish the holiness of a person. I do not discern that such is the biblical style, as admirable as that may happen to be in a worldly sense.

All that I can affirm, apart from complaining about how awkward it is to try to write a book in the situation in which I have found myself recently, is that pain is not a punishment; neither is pain a justification. There are no grounds to be romantic about pain. Pain is a true mystery, so long as this world lasts. Yet it is known that pain is intercessory: one is never alone in pain but is always a surrogate of everyone else who hurts—which is categorically everybody. I consider that this is enough to know if one does trust the Word of God in Judgment.